A PARENT'S SURVIVAL GUIDE TO COLLEGE AND FINANCIAL AID

JIM TRIMBOLI

A Parent's Survival Guide to College and Financial Aid
© James Trimboli 2015
ALL RIGHTS RESERVED

No part of this book may be reproduced or transmitted in any form or by any means, electronic or mechanical, including photocopying, recording or by any information retrieval system.

To order additional copies or for bulk rate information contact the publisher or author. Also available online in electronic format and through industry distribution channels.

Edited by Leslie Turner
leslie@encouragebooks.com

Published and distributed by:

Encourage Publishing, LLC
New Albany, Indiana
812.987.6148
www.encouragebooks.com

ISBN 978-0-9962067-0-9

Printed in the United States

Contents

Foreword and Dedication..4

About the Author..5

Introduction...7

Chapter 1: What to Consider When Choosing a College.......9

Chapter 2: What is Financial Aid? 19

Chapter 3: How is Student Need Determined? 29

Chapter 4: Types of Federal Aid 33

Chapter 5: What Every Student and Parent Needs to
                Know about Student Loans.......................................37

Chapter 6: Budgeting and Building Positive Credit..................49

Chapter 7: Top Ten Most Costly Parent Mistakes......................55

Chapter 8: Other Financial Aid Sources 63

Chapter 9: After Day One 65

Endnotes...67

Additional Resources..69

Foreword

Jim Trimboli's "A Parent's Survival Guide to College and Financial Aid" is a standout resource that gets to the heart of what students and their families need to know when facing two of life's most important decisions: choosing a college and financing a college education.

The book's clear and concise approach displays Trimboli's skill for making a complex process seem far less daunting, in fact, making it quite manageable. This book should be required reading for all families prior to beginning the college decision and financial aid process.

Patricia R. Thompson
Assistant Vice Chancellor
Student Financial Aid Services
State University of New York, System Administration

Dedication

This book is dedicated to my wife and three children, my late mother who always encouraged me to write, and the hard working people in the financial aid industry.

About the Author

Jim Trimboli has been employed in the financial aid industry since 1999, serving as Director of Financial Aid for the State University of New York (SUNY) at Niagara County Community College, located in Sanborn, New York, since 2004.

He holds a Master's Degree in Applied Economics from Buffalo State College as well as an Associate's Degree in Business Management from Bryant & Stratton Business College and a Bachelor's Degree in Business Resource Development from Medaille College. Jim is also SUNY's newest published author as cited by his work in NASFAA's publication "You're The Director: A Guide To Leadership in Student Financial Aid".

Jim also presents regularly at national and regional higher education conferences and is a member of SUNY's Statewide Default Prevention Task Force and Financial Literacy Sub-Committee, which was responsible for statewide procurement that provided financial literacy for students and parents throughout the state of New York.

Jim is past chair of SUNY's Shared Services-Loan Verification Sub-Committee and is a regularly-featured speaker on Financial Wellness and Financial Literacy topics for incoming Niagara County Community College students and parents, local high schools, civic organizations, and other community-sponsored events.

Jim lives in historic Lewiston, New York with his wife, Lisa, and three children, James Jr., Kayley and Alex, and dog Daisy. Jim enjoys fishing in the Lower Niagara River, spending time with his family and working on his six acres of land. He also is very active in coaching youth ice hockey in his local community. Jim has also experienced a parent's perspective and pride as his oldest son entered college in 2011, graduating in 2016.

Introduction

Someone once said "Time is a great thief". Where does the time go? If you're like me it may seem like only yesterday when you brought your child home from the hospital; in a blink of an eye it's now time to send him or her off to college. Over the past eighteen years some of us may have set aside an entire college fund, others may have squirreled away what they could afford, and unfortunately others did not plan on this day arriving so suddenly. Whatever your financial situation may be, this book is sure to help you navigate the daunting task of helping your child fund their education.

I have spent fifteen years of my life working in the financial aid industry. Ten of those years I have been the Director of Financial Aid for a community college that serves over 8,000 students each year. Throughout my years in financial aid I have given countless words of advice to students and their families regarding their financial aid packages, conducted numerous financial aid presentations, and helped numerous students and their families navigate the complicated financial aid process. Oh, did I forget to mention that I am also the parent of a college student? Although the names of the folks I have helped have changed over the years, the look of consternation on the faces of families dealing with planning how to pay for college has not changed. Families and students today are faced with ever increasing tuition costs and decreasing available resources to help offset these costs. The challenge for parents and students alike is to fund a quality education without incurring a heap of debt from which there is no escape.

This book contains information that will help you seamlessly navigate through the complicated financial aid process and give you some particular advice on how to keep college expenses down, help you and your student avoid expensive mistakes and learn easy tips to succeed in college.

My goal for you by the end of this book is to give you peace of mind through the process of funding your child's education and getting them through those first precarious steps of going to college.

Chapter 1
What to Consider When Choosing a College
(So Many Choices, So Little Time!)

What to study

Unfortunately, many students and their families wait until the last minute to decide on what college they want to attend and what course of study they wish to pursue. Parents and their children ideally should begin this conversation no later than the beginning of their son or daughter's junior year of high school. Some may argue that this is too late to begin this discussion; many parents might be pleasantly surprised to find that their child has already begun thinking about which course of study they want to undertake. Even if your child doesn't have a career or field of study in mind, at least you're taking the first steps in a long journey of trying to get your child to do some critical thinking about their future educational goals.

According to a survey conducted in 2006 by New York University's School of Continuing and Professional Studies, "a rarefied group, admittedly, but not necessarily atypical, expected, on average, to change careers three times in their lifetimes, and only 28 percent expected life long careers (1)". College Parents of America states that "It may help parents understand that most college students, some studies suggest a figure as high as 80%, change their major at least once (2)".

By reading the preceding two quotes a parent can reasonably deduct why it is so important to inquire early and often as to what your future college student has in mind. It is better that your child changes his or her mind before they enter a university when it costs nothing, than after they are committed to and enrolled in a field of study. Let's face it: did any of us really know what we wanted to do when we were eighteen years old? Many adults in their thirties and forties still struggle with the career or educational path they want to pursue.

What type of institution

There are many institutions of higher education in this country. There are public and private two year colleges, there are public and private four year universities, and there are technical, trade, business, and community colleges. If that is not enough for one to grasp, there are also graduate and post graduate colleges. To further complicate the issue of choice each one of these options has its own particular price tag.

Next to purchasing a home, a college education is quickly becoming the second largest investment a person can make in their lifetime. The key word is "investment". Unlike other big ticket items you will purchase in your lifetime, a college education is something no one can every take away from you; your degree will never wear out and cannot be traded in or given back. A college education, simply put, is a piece a paper that, coupled with hard work, desire, commitment and dedication, is a license to reach any level of potential in your career field, whether that be personal fulfillment, world-changing accomplishment or even unlimited income. It's not the piece of paper that will make or break you; it's the dedication and effort you put into your degree and the connections you make along the way that will carry you.

Neither does your degree have to be from an Ivy-league or private school to have value. Many students, for example, who started at a community college and continued on at a public university, now earn six figure incomes, thanks to hard work coupled with continued education. Though a solid K-12 education really does help you succeed in college, you may be the valedictorian of your high school with a full scholarship to Harvard and still end up a college drop out. Conversely, you could be an "average" student like most people and truly hit your stride in college. In the game of life there are no guarantees for college students. It's like the old saying "hard work beats talent when talent doesn't work hard". That's why it's so important for college students to make the right choices early on and be committed to their course of study.

Mr. Patrick Banard, high school track coach at Tonawanda High School in Erie County, New York, encouraged his teams with the reminder that the difference between being involved

Case Study: Parents talk about commitment

My wife and I made too much for our child to qualify for any grants that look at financial need, but not enough to send him wherever he wanted to study. We were anxious to help him avoid unnecessary student loan debt, but we had financial limits. We compared college costs and examined our budget early in his senior year of high school. The conversation between my wife and I went something like this. We knew "junior" could succeed academically at any college he desired; however, if he chose the local community college we could afford my wife and I agreed we would pay his full tuition and fees, along with his books. If he decided to attend a different college, we would only pay up to the same amount we had already pledged to come up with for the community college and "junior" would be on the hook for the rest of the other college's cost.

Since there is a limit to how much a student can borrow in a year, this meant certain college choices would be way out of his reach without some significant scholarships. To our amazement, before we could sit him down to have "the talk", "junior" had already figured out on his own it was more economically feasible for him to attend the community college. He made this choice for two reasons. First, he explained he chose the community college because of its program quality and, second, he told us that the community college was much cheaper. He also informed us that along with the cheaper tuition he was able to dually enroll with a local four year university which offered him a $10,000 scholarship in his junior year to transfer to that institution. Once my wife and I picked ourselves off the floor we congratulated him on his wise decision and told him of our payment plan for tuition to offset his costs.

with something and committed to it is like ham and eggs. The chicken is involved while the pig is committed. You should instill that thought into your child throughout the college selection process and do your best to help him assess whether or not he is ready to commit himself fully to his education and to the course of study he selects.

College or not?

It is also important to recognize that a traditional college education isn't for everyone; even a person well-suited for college must be ready for the challenge in order to succeed. Is your child ready? Are they going to the right college for the right reasons? If not, expect some heart-breaking set-backs. All students face obstacles in college; the students least likely to push through those moments often already have one foot out the door because their heart isn't in it. Those same students may point to famously successful college drop-outs like Steve Jobs or Rush Limbaugh as evidence to support a decision to leave college. We can all recognize that these examples are the exception, not the rule, even for the most brilliant students. College is still the best path for long-term career growth and financial stability overall.

However, there are plenty of successful people that work in fields that do not require a college degree, such as the many skilled trade professions. They live productive and happy lives and are gainfully employed. Throughout my higher education career I have seen many parents pressure their children into going to college even though they show no interest or are just not ready. Please don't be "that parent". Though some students do need some strong encouragement, don't push your child toward college, or toward a particular college, for any of the following reasons:

1. He would be the first one in the family to go to college (or fulfill your own dream of a college education)
2. She would graduate from the same school you did, or enter the same profession
3. You want to impress someone else, maintain your family status, or are comparing your child to another student.

These are all roads to disaster. Just because the Joneses sent their cherub to an Ivy League college doesn't mean that your child is ready or wants to go to college. Forcing someone to go to college only leads to failure and an expensive waste of time and money, not to mention the damage it does to your relationship. Further, returning to college at a future date becomes significantly less likely because the first experience was negative.

What we can afford

When selecting a college you want to put all options on the table and evaluate them carefully. The first thing a family must decide on is the cost and how much they can afford out of their household budget. The amount you as a parent are willing to invest should be in balance with your child's commitment to succeed in college and with your own resources. Be careful not to overcommit or make promises you may later regret.

The case study illustrates you should not underestimate the value of your local community college or a four year public institution for a low- priced quality education. As compared to a private institution, public venues of higher education offer a similar product at reasonable prices. When I decided to go back for my Master's in economics later in life, I, too, was faced with a choice. Do I go back to my private pricey college which provided a quality education for my undergraduate degree, or do I go to a public institution that had a similar offering at a cheaper price?

Once I thought about the student loan debt that piled up on me and how it took me eight years to pay it off for my undergraduate work, I decided to give the public institution a shot. It proved to be one of the best decisions I ever made. Not only did I do very well in a tough program, my classes were small and, best of all, I was able to pay for my classes out of pocket rather than amass a pile of student loan debt that would have taken me several years to pay off.

When making the tough choice between sending your child to a public or private college please keep in mind it's not the college that Junior attends that matters as much as it is what your child does while he or she is there. Especially if your child is undecided about declaring a major, it may more advantageous for you to send them to a public college rather than private school in the long run. If your child changes their mind on a course of study it won't end up costing you a small fortune in the end.

Living arrangements

Before you and your child decide on an institution of higher education, you must consider living arrangements. In cases where the college is out-of-state, know the rules for incoming freshmen. Are they required to live on campus? Are you lucky enough to have a willing relative who lives in the area who will provide room and board for your child while they attend college? If they are required to live on campus, is a meal plan required? Make a list of furniture and everything else that your child will need to have while they are away from home. When all is said and done this can lead to an expensive bill on top of the cost of tuition.

Even though living allowances and room and board are considered in most colleges' financial aid packages, it could still add up to be a pretty hefty sum that will require an action plan on your part to decipher a way to fund this amount. If your child is planning to attend a college close to home it might be cheaper for you to help them buy a quality used car or let them take public transportation to commute back and forth to school rather than living on a local campus.

I have heard many parents talk about how they want the college dorm experience for their child at a local campus. This idea must be considered very carefully. Do you really want to encourage your child to take on extra debt so that they can find out what it is like living with several other people they don't know in a dorm room at a local college? Do you want this for them because you never had the opportunity? Or, are you anxious for them to move out for other reasons? Whatever your answer is, you must consider the financial ramifications that come with such a plan.

Books and supplies

The last significant college expense for your child is books and supplies. Once again, most campuses include book and supply allowances in their financial aid budgets; however, these items can add up quickly. When purchasing books and supplies, be a savvy consumer, just as you are with everything else you buy. With just a little forethought you can save yourself a pile of money. For instance, many college bookstores sell used books at about half the price of a new book. Just like other stores, the supply of used books is limited; buy these books early before they are all snapped up.

After your grades post and you know you don't need to repeat the class, you may be able to return the textbook to the bookstore for a small credit, or list your books on a student textbook website to sell them yourself for higher profit. Online websites are often great places to save a lot of money, but beware – returns may be tricky. Many bookstores now offer the wonderful option of renting books. The student simply signs an agreement with the bookstore promising to return the book in good condition at the end of the semester leaving a deposit on a credit card to ensure that the book is brought back in good condition. The bookstore will often e-mail the student a reminder a few days before the book is to be returned. The best part of renting is that the student pays much less than if they purchased books.

Although I don't highly recommend this option, students can also wait until the start of classes to see if the instructor is actually going to use the book. Usually this information is found in the instructor's syllabus. If you are able to contact the instructor beforehand you may want to inquire if the book listed will be required for that particular professor's class. Nothing used to aggravate me more in college then spending a hundred dollars or more on a book and then finding out the first day of class that the instructor decided he or she will not be using the text.

18

Chapter 2
What is Financial Aid?

When I speak to large groups of students and their parents, I often ask this question, "Is financial aid a privilege or an entitlement"? In other words, is it your right to receive financial aid? The first year, if you follow all of the steps and are eligible for a Pell grant, yes; that Pell grant is considered an "entitlement". However, ask any student who is not eligible to apply for financial aid, or who lost their eligibility, and you will learn quickly: receiving financial aid, even student loans, to help pay for college is a privilege, and a student could lose that privilege at any time.

A student can have their aid revoked for many unfortunate situations stemming from poor grades to non-attendance. That's why it is so important that students and parents have a full understanding of what financial aid is and how it works.

Financial aid, in a nutshell, includes any funds that help offset the educational costs for a student who is attending college. Some financial aid is based on need. Other types of financial aid are awarded based on other criteria such as grades. Financial aid can come from several sources which include but are not limited to the following: Federal Government sources, State sources, college sources (also known as institutional aid) and private sources. Within these sources are specific categories that most financial aid falls into which includes grants and scholarships ("free" money), work-study, and loans. Before we get into a description of each specific category of financial aid it is important to know how the federal government defines "need" and how financial need is determined.

Applying for aid – the FAFSA

In order to apply for financial aid (Title IV funds) each student must complete a government form known as a Free Application for Federal Student Aid or FAFSA. The key word in this document is "free". Please be warned that there are many websites or agencies out there that will charge you to complete this form. Though some parents are happy to pay someone to do this and have the money to do so, for most families, this is an unnecessary expense. Some students and their families end up unfortunately spending hundreds of dollars for something they could have done for themselves totally free of charge, often in as little as fifteen minutes. Don't fall into this trap. Applying for the FAFSA is easy and it's FREE.

In fact, it's a lot easier now than when many of today's parents went to college. Until 1997 there was only a paper FAFSA which you had to fill out and "snail mail" to the federal government, then wait about seven to ten weeks to get an answer back via the same "snail mail". Today most FAFSA forms are filed electronically and once you submit your FAFSA you receive an instant federal aid estimate and will have an answer on the amount of financial aid you qualify for sent to your e-mail account within 1-3 business days. .

All you will need is the following free government website to apply for and submit your FAFSA application to the federal government: www.fafsa.gov. At the end of the application, both the student and one parent, if the parent's information is included on the FAFSA, will be required to electronically sign the FAFSA through a secure password you will create through the website and use every year at www.fafsa.gov and other federal financial aid websites.

> **Director's Tip:**
> I always tell students and their families before they start the electronic FAFSA application to think of this process like a family project. First, gather the documentation you will need to complete the FAFSA application. Students will need their Social Security number, alien registration number(if you are not a U.S. citizen), driver's license, most recent W-2 forms, federal income tax returns, bank statements, and any other annual benefit statements. Remember for your son or daughter who is under the age of 24 these documents will be also required for parents.

Parent information on the FAFSA

One of the most frequent questions heard in a financial aid office is, "why do I have to include my parents' information? They are not going to be paying for my education!" Students who are considered "dependent" by the criteria on the FAFSA have to include parent information regardless of whether the parent is paying for their education or supporting the student in any way whatsoever; neither does the U.S. Department of Education consider whether or not the parent claims the student on their tax return, a common misconception.

A dependent student as defined by the Federal Government FAFSA is a student that is under the age of 24 and does NOT meet any of the following criteria for independence:

1. The student is married.
2. The student is currently working on a master's or doctorate program.
3. The student is currently serving on active duty in the U.S. Armed Forces for purposes other than training or is a veteran.
4. The student has children for whom they provide more than half of their support during the upcoming financial aid year.
5. The student has dependents (other than children or spouse) that live with and receive more than have of their support from the student.
6. On or after the student's 13th birthday, both parents were deceased or the student was in foster care or a dependent or ward of the court.
7. The student was considered an emancipated minor, as determined by a court in their state of legal residence.
8. The student was under court-ordered legal guardianship, as determined by the court in their state of legal residence.
9. At any time on or after July 1 of the current tax year for FAFSA purposes the student was determined to be an unaccompanied youth who was homeless or self-supporting and at risk of being homeless(4) by:
   1. Their high school or school district homeless liaison,
   2. The director of an emergency shelter or transitional housing program funded by the U.S. Department of Housing and Urban Development, or
   3. The director of a runaway youth basic center or transi-

tional living program

If a dependent student meets any one of the rubrics stated above, the student can file as an independent student. What this means for mom or dad is that they do not have to provide any of their information on the FAFSA, nor do they have to sign it. Their child will be using only their own information to complete the FAFSA and only have to provide their income information unless they were married, in which case their spouse's income and information would have to be included as well.

If a student who is under the age of 24 claims to qualify to be independent under the above criteria, that student may be required to bring documentation to the financial aid office that supports this claim. Examples of documents that may be required for submission by the financial office include but are not limited to: death certificates, marriage certificates, proof of emancipation or legal guardianship, military DD214 forms, IRS transcripts, and letters on high school or agencies' letterheads.

Please keep in mind that the financial aid office only asks for these documents when required to do so by the federal government. The financial aid office is only a conduit between the student and the federal government. Remember, it's the federal government's money; it doesn't belong to the student, the parent or the school, so whatever the federal government requires, the financial aid office must receive. Put simply, you will not receive your aid package until you comply with the government's requests.

One example of documentation that is often a source of contention with students is when a student who is under age 24 has a child or children of their own. In a case like this the student has to be able to prove that they support themselves and provide more than 50% of their children's support. A student in this scenario must live on their own and have enough income to support their children.

The best rule of thumb when it comes to questions about whether a student under the age of 24 can be considered as an independent student is to speak with a qualified financial aid officer at the school the student plans to attend. In some circumstances, a student who would otherwise have to include parent information and get their signature may qualify for a dependency appeal if there are unique circumstances preventing them from getting their parent's help.

FAFSA deadlines and details

When should the FAFSA be completed? New FAFSA applications for the upcoming year will be available online every year starting January 1st. Every state has its own deadline for students to qualify for state aid and there is a "Deadlines" link at www.fafsa.gov where you may look up the filing deadline for your own state.

State deadlines usually only matter if the student plans to attend college in the state where they, and their parents, legally reside; however, some colleges may use the state deadline for their own scholarship deadline. Review your college's website or contact the financial aid office to see if they have an earlier FAFSA filing deadline or require an additional application to be considered for other scholarships. Ideally, to allow a college proper time to process your student aid package and FAFSA, every student should try to complete the FAFSA by the state deadline, but no later than April 1st.

Case Study: Students under age 24 with children
Let's look at Jessica and her daughter, Claire. Jessica and Claire live rent-free in a separate apartment in her parents' basement. Jessica works part-time and only earns about $2000 per year. Claire receives healthcare benefits through a county agency. When completing the FAFSA, Jessica's parents' information would be required, but both Jessica and Claire would be included in the number in the household.

What if Jessica and Claire moved in with Claire's father, Gabe? Since Jessica and Gabe are not married and Gabe is supporting all three, Jessica would still have to include her parents' information on the FAFSA, even if they did not support her at all nor claim her on their tax return.

If Jessica and Gabe get married, Jessica's parent information will not be required on the following year's FAFSA, but Gabe's information will be required. Jessica and Gabe could file a special circumstance appeal for change in marital status through the office of financial aid if they marry during the school year, but this does not always guarantee more grant funding.

     A student and their family can complete the FAFSA after April 1st; in fact, students can complete the FAFSA long after classes have begun and still receive aid for those classes, provided the academic term has not ended. However please keep in mind that all FAFSA applications from every student in the nation are processed by the Department of Education in the order that they receive them and forwarded to each college the student lists on the FAFSA.

Colleges often receive high volumes of FAFSA's in late spring through late summer which slows their response time, especially if the student is required to submit additional paperwork. The longer a student waits to the send the application in, the longer the wait will be to receive an answer back on how much aid you will be receiving. If you want your aid ready before classes begin, file before April 1st.

> **Director's Tip:**
> I always tell my students to file or update their FAFSA online two weeks after their parents and they file their tax returns. If you mail your tax returns in, you'll need to wait 6-8 weeks. Once your tax returns are in the IRS database, the FAFSA interface can pull the correct tax information straight from the IRS website, ensuring accurate information and significantly reducing the chances you'll have to go through a sometimes lengthy process called "verification".

For students worried about missing the state deadline, the FAFSA can be filed before tax returns are completed, simply by using estimates and the previous year's tax returns as a guideline. Once tax returns are completed, wait a few weeks then go back to the FAFSA to import your updated tax information straight from the IRS through the link for making corrections.

I have already mentioned that the FAFSA stands for Free Application for Student Aid. You are applying for free grant money from the U. S. Department of Education using this form. Grant money available under the FAFSA includes the Pell Grant, Supplemental Educational Opportunity Grant (SEOG), the

TEACH grant and the Work Study award. I will discuss these in full detail in the next chapter.

Basically, the Pell and SEOG grants are "free" money for a student to put toward offsetting the cost of attending college. Though all federal grants and loans are awarded from the government based on household income and need, the neediest students (low income students) as deemed by the federal government are awarded these two particular types of grants.

Often students will say to me that they don't have to fill out the FAFSA because their parents make too much money. I remind these students that if they wish to apply for a low-interest federal student loan they are required to fill out the FAFSA. Federal government Title IV regulations allow students to borrow a limited amount of low interest student loans every year without a credit check. Some colleges also require the student to fill out the FAFSA application in order to apply for scholarships.

Students and families needing help to complete their FAFSA can call 1-800-433-3243 for assistance or visit **www.collegegoalsundayusa.org** to find dates and times of free events held throughout their state and staffed by financial aid professionals, just to help families complete the FAFSA.

To help make applying for financial aid via the online FAFSA much easier, the Department of Education and The Department of the Internal Revenue have joined forces. The new process is referred to as the IRS retrieval tool which is embedded in the electronic FAFSA application. Electronic tax return files can wait approximately two weeks after filing their electronic tax returns via the IRS. Once the IRS processes the tax returns, students can log on to the FAFSA website and download the required IRS tax information right into the FAFSA.

The IRS download will not only make completing the electronic FAFSA faster and easier, it also may help students avoid the verification process which would require the student to bring additional documents into the financial aid office in order for the student to receive their financial aid package. Additional verification can be avoided by double checking data entry errors on the electronic FAFSA before signing and submitting the FAFSA. Some common data entry errors are as follows:
- Social Security Numbers
- Divorced/remarried parent information
- Parents/stepparent's earned income
- Untaxed income
- U.S. income taxes paid
- Household size
- Number in postsecondary education
- Real estate and investment net worth

Students and their parents, remember: there are companies and websites that will file FAFSA forms for a fee. You can file this form yourself at no cost. FAFSA is short for **FREE** Application for Federal Student Aid.

Chapter 3
How Is Student Need Determined?

Now that you have helped your student submit their FAFSA, you're probably wondering about the next steps.

The financial data that a student submits on their FAFSA is then processed by the Department of Education via something called a "needs methodology formula". "FAFSA methodology formula is used by the government to calculate the expected family contribution and to estimate the student's financial aid package (6)." This needs-based financial aid formula evaluates and determines the family's ability to pay for educational costs.

Financial aid is a limited resource so in essence this formula determines who the neediest of students are based on household size, income and certain assets. The formula that the federal government uses to determine need is:

Cost of Attendance (COA)
- Expected Family Contribution (EFC)
= Financial Need

In order to understand how this formula works, we must break down each component of this formula to gain an understanding of exactly what the government is looking at to determine what goes into the cost of a student going to college and what items are considered by the government to offset what a family is expected to pay for their son or daughter to attend an institution of higher education. The cost of attendance to a college includes the following:

- Tuition and fees
- Room and board
- Books and supplies
- Transportation
- Miscellaneous personal expenses

COA may also be increased to include:

- Loan fees
- Study abroad costs
- Dependent care and dependent tuition expenses
- Expenses related to a disability
- Purchase of education-related technology

Director's Tip:
Many first-year students are under the misconception that if they qualify for a Pell grant all of their expenses will be covered, including housing. Since the amount of Pell grant a student receives does not vary school by school, this cannot be true; in most cases a full Pell grant will not even be enough to cover all of the basic tuition, fees and books, except perhaps at some public community colleges. This is why it is so important to know the costs up front.

All of the previous expenses are what a college calculates to be in a student's budget for the year. In essence, the college's COA considers what the typical student's expected expenses will be from various sources within the academic year. The COA is just an estimate and is not a good indicator of the actual bill. It is used to establish a maximum amount of aid any one student may receive during one year of college, but also does not imply the student will receive that much aid.

The second part of this formula examines the student's expected family contribution, or EFC for short. All sources of a student's family income and assets that were reported on their FAFSA are examined in this process. This formula also looks at your household family size and how many family members are in college or a career school. The lower the family household income and the greater the number of family members in college, the higher a family's need for financial aid is.

Please also note that the EFC will stay the same regardless of the college selected. In a nutshell, the EFC is all about what the government deems is a fair amount that the family should be able to provide that year in order to help cover the cost of the student's education. Families are never required to pay a student's bill, and including parent information on the FAFSA in no way obligates the parent to pay for the student's education. This is a common fear among parents. Only the student is responsible for the cost of their education.

The EFC also does not necessarily represent the amount a student will literally have to pay the school and does not mean the government will be able to cover the rest of the bill. In most cases, families are already providing room and board, transportation and personal expenses, for example, and the student would have to pay the school only the amount of the bill not covered by the student's financial aid. Still, it stands to reason that a school with a higher COA is going to have a higher bill to pay as well, and a family with a low EFC is going to have more financial aid available to help offset that bill.

The following chart illustrates how the needs formula could impact a student's cost of attending college.

Examples of EFC and Need

	College A	College B	College C
COA	$5,500	$30,000	$60,000
minus EFC	- $5,000	- $5,000	- $5,000
Financial need	$500	$25,000	$55,000

This chart can be used as a guide to help a parent and a student navigate through college expense and their personal finances in order to come up with a game plan to help offset the expense of going to college. It will also help students and their families determine which colleges are affordable options and which institutions of higher education may be out of their financial reach.

Chapter 4
Types of Federal Aid

This chapter will cover the types of federal financial aid that are available and the criteria that make a student and their families eligible for grants and student loans. Please remember that it is a government requirement that a student and their family complete the FAFSA in order to begin the process of qualifying for these federal aid programs.

Pell Grant

"The Pell Grant is named after former Rhode Island Senator Claiborne Pell, as he sponsored a bill to help fund low and moderate income students so they could attend college(7)". The Pell grant, like any other grant fund, is "free" money based on household income and assets that a student does not have to pay back. The Pell Grant award amount is based on COA, EFC and enrollment status. A student must be registered in a degree or certificate program and be enrolled in at least one class. The student must also maintain good academic standing according to their school's criteria in order to receive the award again.

Once the student receives a bachelor's degree or receives the equivalent of six years of Pell payments they are no longer eligible to receive the Pell Grant. To see the most recent annual Pell grant award for students attending full-time, visit www.studentaid.ed.gov.

FSEOG Grant

FSEOG stands for the "Supplemental Educational Opportunity Grant". This grant is awarded first to those students with exceptional financial need who have the lowest EFCs at their institutions. Priority in awarding this grant is also given to students that are Pell eligible. To see the most current maximum annual FSEOG grant award visit www.studentaid.ed.gov.

Please note that the FSEOG is known as a campus-based program. This means that the campus you are attending has to participate and apply for this type of aid every year, and the award amount and criteria vary by school. The amount of FSEOG that each campus receives from the federal government is limited and can vary from year to year. Consequently, schools often run out of these funds in any given year. This is why it is important that you apply for your FAFSA early so you can ensure your award of FSEOG if you qualify.

Federal Work Study

Federal Work Study is also considered a campus-based program, so it is also essential with this program that you submit the FAFSA as early as possible, since funds can be limited. The student does not necessarily have to be eligible for a Pell grant to receive this award. The Federal Work Study program allows students to be employed on or off campus with part-time jobs. Students receive a regular paycheck for hours worked during the academic year, up to the total of their work study award amount. This program is offered to both undergraduate and graduate students.

Personally I can't think of a better type of employment for a student for a plethora of reasons. First, work study is a very good way for a student to gain valuable work experience in higher education. A student can gain real life experiences working in various offices on campus. Another good reason to pursue a work study position is convenience. Students in many cases can work the hours they want and may want to fill in free time between classes. Students who work on campus also don't have to worry about the costs of transportation to and from work or about an employer requiring them to work during class time.

Please keep in mind that work study payments cannot generally be deducted from a tuition bill and must be paid in form a salary, though, in some schools, the bursar may be able to withhold payment at the student's request and apply it to the student's bill. An added benefit of work-study is that income earned through work-study and declared as such on the FAFSA will not be included in the formula used to determine the student's EFC for the following year.

TEACH Grant-

The TEACH Grant is a relatively new grant program first offered by the U. S. Department of Education in 2007. TEACH stands for Teacher Education Assistance for College and Higher Education. In short, the TEACH Grant can provide free money up to $4,000 per year to students who plan to pursue a curriculum in the teaching profession. The savvy student should be aware that, upon applying for the TEACH Grant, he or she must sign a TEACH Grant contract which requires the student to serve and teach students in a high needs field for a least four academic years, within eight years of graduation or ceasing enrollment in the course of study as required by the grant.

All students thinking about applying for the TEACH Grant should fully understand that failure to complete all stipulations and requirements of the TEACH Grant will result in all TEACH Grant funds received under this program being converted to a Direct Unsubsidized Student Loan. For this reason, students and their families need to be prudent and ask the financial aid office at the college where they are attending for a copy of the regulations regarding the Teach Grant so students and their families can review these very carefully before obligating themselves to the grant. Please note that not all colleges offer the TEACH Grant so check with your financial aid office for availability.

Chapter 5

What Every Student and Parent Needs to Know about Student Loans

When I give my financial aid lectures, I spend the most time discussing the importance of understanding student loans to both parents and students. Over the years, I have been asked more questions about this topic than any other. One of the most important facts that parents and students alike should know about loans is that loans are not free money like grants, and students and parents who borrow education loans need to pay these loans back. The nation's student loan debt burden now exceeds one trillion dollars, reportedly more than the nation's credit card debt (8)."

We have all seen the articles in papers and magazines on the increasing student loan debt and the effect the debt load has on students, their families, and institutions of higher learning. For the student, these loans are an awesome responsibility. Student loans are not subject to a credit check and are readily accessible at almost every college in America. This fact alone may put a careless student loan borrower in serious financial jeopardy.

> **Director's Tip:**
> Students never have to borrow the full amount of student loans offered. Loans can be reduced to just what a student needs and increased later if needed. Also, the full amount of the loan is not available up front, but usually split evenly between academic terms, a common misstep by students who expect the full amount will apply to their first bill.

The loan process

I will be discussing the many types of student loans available to students a little later in this chapter. However, before discussing the terms and conditions of those loans, it is import that you are aware of the process you will go through in order to obtain a student loan.

All federal student loans require a student to perform some type of loan counseling. Known as the "entrance counseling session", most schools ask students to go to the Department of Education's website, www.studentloans.gov, also available through the link found at www.direct.ed.gov.

Both websites are dedicated to the subject of federal student loans. For their first loan, students must complete an online tutorial that provides useful tips and tools to help students manage and develop a budget for their educational expenses and think about their borrowing. In addition, it will provide students with a full understanding of what student loans are and a full disclosure of their rights and responsibilities when borrowing student loans. Please remember that if the student plans to take out a student loan it is a requirement that they complete the FAFSA application first.

Once they complete their entrance interview it is now time for them to complete what is known as the electronic Master Promissory Note (MPN). This too can be completed at www.studentloans.gove or www.direct.ed.gov. The MPN is a legal document that explains the terms and conditions of the loan and commits the student to repay the loan and any interest and fees to the Department of Education when the time comes. To complete the MPN the student will need some pertinent information, which includes but is not limited to the following items:
- Student name
- Address
- Date of Birth
- Social Security Number
- Name and contact information of two references
- Signature

Once the student completes the MPN and signs it, they are promising the U.S. Department of Education they will pay the loan back. It is extremely important that the parents do not take it upon themselves to complete the entrance counseling and MPN steps for their student. First, it is against the law to do so. Second, the student must be fully aware they are taking out a loan that must be repaid, by them, which will show up on their credit report as well. Many students and parents have broken relationships because the parent, typically with good intentions, took out a loan without the student's knowledge or understanding.

After the student signs the MPN, the college will certify their loan via the federal government. The funds will then be sent electronically to the institution and will apply to the student's bill as early as ten days before or as late as thirty days after the first day of the enrollment period, depending on the school's loan disbursement policy.

Things students must consider before borrowing

Some thoughts have probably crossed your mind by now. What if the student can't pay their loans back after they graduate? What if they can't find a job? What if they didn't like the quality of their education? Regardless of what their situation is after they graduate, your child is required to pay their loans back.

Typically there is a 6 month deferment period that the government grants them once they either graduate, fall below 6 credit hours in their current program of study, or withdraw from college. This deferment period is designed to give students time to enroll in another program of study (which means the loan will go back into "in-school" deferment) or give the student enough time to find a job to start paying on their loan balances. Not paying on a student loan is not a wise option. As they will see, if the student fails to pay on a student loan there can be some very serious ramifications for them.

As a student loan borrower there are two different situations that can jeopardize their financial future. The first situation is known as delinquency. A student loan is considered delinquent if a payment has not been received the day after the payment due date. Just like car loans, home loans, or personal loans, student loans need to be paid on time in order to keep your student out of financial trouble.

Often, people take a lackadaisical approach to student loans, as they view them as unimportant when compared to mortgage loans, car loans, or any type of collateralized loan. People tend to pay for loans that they think are more important. When in financial trouble, borrowers tend to pay first on loans when they know that the items attached to them can be repossessed or foreclosed on. This is an unfortunate practice as student loans are different from most unsecured loans in many ways, as you will see.

> **Director's Tip:**
> Parents, don't be tempted to promise your student you will pay off their student loans once they graduate. You may not be able or willing to do so when the time comes and your student will not appreciate their adverse credit report and mounting debt they alone are responsible for paying.

The second situation that can occur on a student loan is known as default. Default occurs at 270 days of delinquency on a student loan. This means that the government now deems the student's delinquent loan as bad debt and they will be subject to the following ramifications in an effort to collect their defaulted loan:

- Reported to Credit Bureaus
- Income tax refunds and other Federal payments withheld
- Lottery winnings withheld
- Wages can be garnished
- Professional license may not be renewed (such as Nursing or Cosmetologist)
- Not eligible for future Federal financial aid

- Not eligible for certain Federal benefits
- They will be responsible for all debt collection costs
- They will be sued for the balance they owe

Student borrowers should also know that student loans are exempt from bankruptcy, so if they cannot pay their student loans there is no protection for them under bankruptcy law.

My reasoning for discussing student loan default and delinquency first was not meant to scare you or prevent your student from borrowing student loans; it was meant to make sure they are educated and savvy borrowers. The grim reality is that most students will have to borrow a student loan at some point during their college education. It is important for students to understand and recognize how student loans work and what pitfalls should be avoided.

Types of loans

Now that you as a parent are aware of the great responsibilities your student will undertake when borrowing a student loan it is time to take a look at what types of loans are available for a student to borrow to help offset the cost of a college education. In a nutshell, there are five basic types of student loans available to a student and their families to offset the cost of school.

Perkins Loan

This low interest loan is granted to undergraduate or graduate students with exceptional need. Availability of this loan may be limited, and not all colleges participate in the Federal Perkins Loan Program. The criteria and maximum loan limit is up to $5,500 for an undergraduate or up to $8,000 for a graduate student, as determined by the policies of the school. The Perkins Loan program has a fixed 5% interest rate and has a separate entrance counseling and MPN process. This program may not be available in the future.

Federal Direct Subsidized Loan

This loan is awarded to students with exceptional need. As of 2015, freshman students could receive a loan amount up to $3,500, sophomores, $4,500 and juniors and seniors could receive up to $5,500 per year up to a maximum of $23,000.

The term "subsidized" means that the interest on these student loans will be paid by the government while the borrower is in school at least half time. This historically low fixed interest rate is reset for new loans annually based on the prime interest rate, and can be found at www.studentloans.gov.

Federal Direct Subsidized loans also have a six month deferment period that begins after the student stops attending college, falls below half time or graduates. This deferment period is to help a student prepare for repayment of their loans via giving the student some time to find a job or make arrangements to repay their loans.

It is important to understand that due to recent Department of Education changes students can only borrow a Federal Direct Subsidized for a maximum of a 150% of their time frame of study. In other words, for a student who attends a two year college pursuing a two year degree, that student can only receive up to three years of a subsidized loan. After the third year that student would no longer be able to borrow a subsided loan as long as they continue to attend a two-year institution or pursue a two-year program.

The same would be true for a four-year college; however the maximum time frame to receive a subsidized student loan would be 6 years. For one-year certificate programs the loss of subsidy would occur after a year and a half.

> **Director's Tip:**
> My simple rule of thumb when it comes to borrowing loans is, if you don't have to borrow a student loan, then don't. If you do have to borrow a loan, be a savvy, educated loan borrower and borrow only the amount you need. Being educated and savvy means knowing exactly what borrowing a student loan entails and reading everything about your loan terms before taking out student loans.

Federal Direct Unsubsidized Loan

This loan is non need-based and a dependent student can borrow up to $2,000 a year, more if they do not qualify for the full amount of subsidized loans. This amount may be increased for independent students or for those students whose parents are denied a Parent PLUS loan. (If your Parent PLUS loan application was denied, the student should seek out help from their college financial aid office.)

Beginning in 2015, interest on unsubsidized student loans matches the subsidized loan interest rate but, unlike subsidized loans, accrues immediately (visit www.studentloans.gov for current rates). Federal Direct Unsubsidized loans also have a six-month deferment period after the student stops attending college, falls below half time or graduates before they must begin repaying their loans.

Parent Plus loans

In order to qualify for a parent PLUS loan, you must be the legal parent of a dependent undergraduate student. You do not have to be the custodial parent nor the parent listed on the FAFSA to apply. Please note that a credit check is required on the parent for this type of loan. In order to receive this loan the parent must not have an adverse credit history, although requirements have been relaxed and an appeal process is in place, allowing parents to be approved often under somewhat adverse credit conditions.

The loan amount will be determined by the college based on the institution's cost of attendance minus any other aid the student is receiving. Parent PLUS loan interest rates and an application link can be found at www.studentloans.gov. Repayment of Parent PLUS loans begins in 60 days unless the parent chooses to defer their payment in sync with the student's loan deferment.

Non-government Private Loan or Alternative Loan

The term 'private' means that these loans come from private banks or lenders. You should also be aware that some colleges do not participate in the private loan programs. Students can borrow up to the cost of attendance less any financial aid received. Any applicant for a private loan will be required to pass certain income criteria and a credit check. Private loans also may not have an interest rate cap, may have variable interest rates and a cosigner may be required.

> **Director's Tip:**
> I would strongly suggest that students use private or alternative loans only as a last resort. All students qualify for Direct student loans, which generally have much better interest rates and terms than private loans, unless the student has poor academic standing or has borrowed the maximum possible in Direct student loans.

Finally, when the student's repayment period begins, private loans cannot be consolidated with federal Direct loans into the same lump payment and do not have terms and conditions as favorable as federal Direct loans.

My best advice to students and their families is to only borrow what you need. Although it may not be the most interesting reading in the world, it is a good idea to read all parts of your loan agreement before you sign it. Be sure you understand the exact loan terms that you are agreeing to.

REMEMBER, LOANS NEED TO BE PAID BACK! Most repayment terms of Federal Student loans require a ten year repayment plan with a minimum of a $50.00 a month payment.

There are programs through the military, the federal government and a variety of private and public organizations to pay student loans off as a benefit. Though this can be a great help, be careful – each of these offers comes with an obligation on the student's part, often to work a certain number of years, and requires strict adherence to the rules. Above all, do not increase your borrowing unnecessarily just because there is a future promise from a third party to pay those loans off.

    Don't advise your student to take on a mountain of debt, just because it is "easy" money; they could quickly ruin their financial future. Students with high student loan debt often have great trouble after college being approved for a mortgage or car loan, or may have fewer career options due to their debt obligation. Teach them how to live like a student today so they don't have to live like one for the rest of their life, simply because they immersed themselves in a pile of debt from which there is no escape.

Chapter 6

Budgeting and Building Positive Credit

It's almost impossible for a student to be able to make good borrowing decisions without some basic understanding of budgeting and their all-important credit history. Unfortunately, many students enter college already in debt, or having worked throughout high school with nothing to show for their hard work due to poor spending and saving habits. Often, college is the first time students have to really think about having enough money to buy food or gas, keeping a checking account balanced or navigating their way through unscrupulous offers of credit from car lots, retailers, credit card companies and online financial predators anxious to get their private information.

Budgeting

In order to understand the economics of education, one must understand what a budget is and, more importantly, how to live by one. Let's face it: we can't spend more money than we earn without getting into financial trouble. A budget, simply put, is living within your economic means. Your student must know the difference between a "want" and a "need". Your student may want a million dollar mansion and a Corvette, but what they really need is affordable housing and reliable transportation.

> *Case Study:*
> *The cost of minimum credit card payments*
>
> *Teach your student that they should never charge more in a month than they can repay within the month. Maintaining a credit card balance over time can cost them in the long run.*
>
> *This example illustrates how long it can take to pay off a $2000 balance on a credit card and how expensive it can be to only pay the minimum due.*
>
> *$2,000 purchase on 15% interest card*
> *$30.00 per month minimum payment*
>
> *Time to pay off: 11 years and 8 months*
> *(with no additional purchases to card)*
>
> *Total repayment cost: $4,200*
> *(the $2,000 original purchase and $2,200 in interest)*

Here are some interesting debt facts:
- The average household carried a balance of $15.611 on credit cards as of December 2014.
- In 2014 Americans owed more than $882.6 billion on credit cards (9).

- Only 14% of freshman students have credit cards, while the average credit card balance in 2014 of all students was $499.
- In 2013 students charged an annual average of $3,156, 62% paying their balances in full each month. (10)

Every parent should insist that their son or daughter create their own monthly budget program. There are many interactive programs available to students to accomplish this very task. One of my favorites is www.cashcourse.org. On sites such as CashCourse students can create their own monthly budget and find other useful financial information such as: understanding the financial aid process, what to look for in renting an apartment, understanding taxes and banking, and even how to talk to parents about money.

Whatever budgeting program your child will use, it is important that they track and categorize their monthly spending and income. In their budgets they should not only allow for fixed costs but should also plan for unexpected expenses.

> **Director's Tip:**
> If your student does not have a job, they should not have a credit card, since they have no way to pay their bill. Students should absolutely not plan on using their financial aid to pay their credit card bill. Instead, they should deposit financial aid refunds in a safe place and draw out funds when educational expenses come up.

A savvy student will always look for ways to cut expenses. Help your student reduce costs using some of the methods listed below:
- Live with parents when possible instead of living on campus.
- If you are not required to live on campus, see if there are less expensive housing units close to campus and consider sharing the cost with a roommate.
- Eat at home or in the campus dining hall or learn to cook instead of eating out at restaurants.
- Don't overspend on travel and entertainment.
- Use the college computer lab instead of buying a computer.
- Buy or rent used text books.
- Buy used furniture.
- Try to carpool.
- Get a part-time job.

Getting a job serves two purposes: you can earn extra money, and you have less time to spend it. If you qualify for work study jobs on campus take advantage of this benefit as you will not have to travel back and forth to work.

Students should also get in the habit of maintaining files for their student loan documents and billing statements. This will help students stay informed on what they owe and help them track monthly payments.

Helping your student build positive credit

Many students are under the mistaken impression that taking out a student loan helps build a positive credit history. In truth, taking out loans hurts their credit until years later when they start to pay those loans back, and if they ever miss a payment or only pay the minimum, that debt will hurt their credit, not help it.

I recommend that each student have no more than one credit card if they want to build a positive credit history. However, because of the federal CARD Act of 2009, many students under age 21 will need a co-signer to qualify for their own credit card, often a parent. Remember that co-signing on your student's card also reflects on the co-signer's credit.

Students should pay cash when they can, and only charge items that they need. It is also important that students pay off their credit card balances every month and avoid late payments and fees.

The spending and borrowing habits your student establishes in college will greatly affect their lifestyle after college, including where they live, what they drive, their personal relationships, and their everyday financial options.

Helping your student avoid predatory creditors

College students don't like to think of themselves as vulnerable, but we know that they are susceptible to all sorts of temptations, including unethical people and companies trying to part them from their money.

Before you send your student off to college, arm them with some basic rules to live by:

1. Never sign anything at a car lot without an experienced and trusted advisor to help you negotiate and look for bet-

ter offers or terms. That sweet ride may be tempting, but repairing your old car may make more sense right now.
2. Never give verbal agreement to anything nor any private information over the phone. Don't trust anyone who asks you for that information.
3. Shred unwanted credit applications and monitor your credit throughout the year for identity theft.
4. Learn how to balance your checking account and monitor it at least weekly for unauthorized debits.
5. Stay away from revolving accounts offered by retailers. They hurt your credit and lead to unnecessary spending.

Chapter 7
Top Ten Most Costly Parent Mistakes

With all good intention, sometimes parents make very costly mistakes when it comes to helping their child pay for college. Here are the most common or most expensive mistakes every financial aid office has seen parents make:

1. **Having the student move out**
   Don't make plans for that extra room just yet – living on their own does not mean your information will not be required on the FAFSA, and living at home is one of the easiest ways to trim college costs. In fact, make sure your student has a quiet place to study at home, preferably with stable Internet access.

2. **Emancipating the student**
   Some divorce decrees stipulate the student will be 'emancipated' on their 18th birthday. This does not mean they can

answer "yes" to the emancipation question on the FAFSA. Parent information is still required. Once a student reaches the age of majority in their state, usually age 18, they are no long considered a minor; emancipation at this point is expensive and useless as far as financial aid is concerned.

3. Using the wrong parent(s) on the FAFSA

Students do not get to choose which parent to use on the FAFSA, in cases where the parents are divorced, separated or remarried. Here are the rules:

1. The student always uses the parent with whom they live or where they last lived the most. If that parent is remarried, the spouse's information is included, even if they have a pre-nuptial agreement absolving the new spouse from education expenses. Even though many parents claim to have a 50/50 shared custody agreement, financial aid officers will tell you there is no such thing as a 50/50 split; someone always pays more, either by carrying the insurance or in some other way. The student generally knows who this is.
2. If the student's parents, biological or adoptive, are not married but live together, both parents must be on the FAFSA.
3. If the parent's marriage is legal anywhere in the world, both people must be included on the FAFSA.
4. If the parents split after the student moved out, the student uses the parent that most recently provided the highest amount of support.

Correcting this error after the fact is often difficult and costly, forcing the student to repay funds they have received or find ways to cover an unexpected bill late in the academic term.

4. Miscounting the number of household members or number in college

Parents often don't realize they can include older children not living at home in the household number on the FAFSA, provided that sibling would have to include the same parent information on their FAFSA, should they decide to go to college. You can also include grandparents who have moved in, or anyone, regardless of age, relative or not, living on your property, as long as you are providing more than 50% of their support.

The number in the household going to college can also be confusing. Parents cannot be counted in this number, though any of the other household members can, even if they do not live at home. The student is always counted in the household, even if he doesn't live at home.

5. Cashing out retirement

Many parents are tempted to cash out their retirement to pay for "Junior's" college. Not only will you be required to pay a hefty tax on that early cash-out, but you are putting your future financial stability in jeopardy, which will eventually come back to burden your children. Avoid this expensive option at all costs.

6. Refusing to provide information on the FAFSA

Sometimes parents refuse to provide information on the FAFSA, perhaps because 1) they don't trust the government or the school, 2) they don't understand why it is required, 3) they are afraid their tax returns will be audited, 4) they do not want their student to know what they earn or are not getting along with them, or 5) the parent does not have a legal Social Security number.

> ## Case Study: Who's in the Household?
>
> *Ramone lives at home with his parents, grandparents, his 27-year-old sister Celia and her baby, and his Aunt Gloria, all of whom are supported by his father and mother. He has an older brother, Enrique, age 23, who lives on his own, is not married or in the military and has no children, and another sister, Julia, age 28, who also lives on her own.*
>
> *Both of his sisters and his mother are also enrolled in college, working toward their own degrees.*
>
> *Ramone's household includes 9 people (Ramone, his two parents, his two grandparents, his aunt, his sister Celia and her child, and his brother, Enrique).*
>
> *Two members are counted as "in college" on the FAFSA (Ramone and Celia). Julia is not in the household or number in college because she is over 24 and not living at home. Parents cannot be included in the number in college.*

The truth is, the Department of Education never shares information with the IRS, and only receives information from the IRS if the parent or student give permission. FAFSA compliance does not trigger tax return audits, and parents without Social Security numbers can enter all 9's in place of this number without fear.

If parents refuse to help with the FAFSA the student is ineligible for any aid at all, and can only get a loan if the parent signs a separate letter of refusal. The best way to address these concerns is to make an appointment to visit the financial aid officer at your college.

7. **Misstating assets on the FAFSA**
   If parents are required to enter a value for their assets on the FAFSA, they should not include their family home and personal belongings or cars. They should not include any retirement assets such as 401K or IRA accounts or other retirement savings.

   Parents living on and working a family farm should not include the value of this farm. Small business owners with less than 100 employees should not include the value of their business assets.

   Do you own a second home? The liquidation value of that property should be included. Did you cash out a 401K? It will show on your tax return as taxable income – don't add it to this question as well. Did you convert a traditional retirement IRA to a Roth IRA? This will be included in your Adjusted Gross Income on the FAFSA, but you can file a special circumstance appeal with the office of financial aid to have it removed.

8. **Not involving the student in the financial process**
   When parents "take care" of their adult children by completing and signing legal documents on their behalf as they have been in the habit of doing, the student never learns to watch for important messages and deadlines, and often does not realize they have a bill to pay or a loan taken out in their name. Parents don't get those important messages and cannot call in

for information due to FERPA laws (Family Education Right to Privacy Act); consequently, bills go unpaid, fees mount and students lose out.

> **Director's Tip:**
> Never deliberately enter false information on the FAFSA, even if a professional recommends it. Bad advice comes from everywhere, but costs for this error could be high.
>
> The U.S. Department of Education compares FAFSA data year to year and financial aid professionals are required to audit discrepancies and correct or cancel aid if needed, as well as report known fraud.
>
> The statement both parent and student agree to at the end of the FAFSA application states "If you purposely give false or misleading information, you may be fined up to $20,000, sent to prison, or both."

9. **Expecting the student to work too many hours**
   Parents, often anxious to see their children take on adult responsibility, sometimes do not appreciate the work required to succeed in college, particularly if the parent has never attended, and expect their student to work whenever they are not in class. A little work is good – a lot of work can cause a student to fail or have to repeat expensive classes. For every one credit hour taken, a student should reserve three hours each week to complete class assignments and study. A student attending 15 hours will need 45 hours a week or more for class work.

Talk to your student well ahead of time about your worries and the limits of your ability to support them. Help them set reasonable work hours with plenty of schedule gaps for unexpected situations, and if they can't work as much, they may need a little cash now and then. Establishing boundaries and expectations ahead of time helps everyone make good decisions.

10. Letting the student miss important deadlines

Sometimes parents are too "hands-off" when it comes to financial aid. Many students are still learning to take care of things themselves that their parent has always done for them.

Meeting deadlines may be the one area parents should be hyper-vigilant about. Don't let your students miss important deadlines. Especially for students who are fully Pell-eligible, missing a state deadline could easily mean the difference between having their entire bill covered and having a large bill to worry about.

Missing a scholarship deadline could cost ongoing benefits as renewable scholarships go to other students. This is too high a price to pay for teaching your child responsibility. In some states the FAFSA must be filed as early as January 1 to qualify for state aid. Remember, you don't need to have taxes complete to file the FAFSA. Help your student file using estimates and use the FAFSA tax return import feature a few weeks after you have filed. Most students need parents' personal and income information as well as a parent's electronic signature on their FAFSA.

Students should start working on scholarship applications early, well before the time comes to file the FAFSA, and often must do so every year. Scholarship deadlines are posted on the school or organization website or on the actual application.

In addition, your school may have priority deadlines for completing any extra paperwork that is required to receive financial aid. Often those papers require parent information and a signature. Miss those deadlines and your child may at minimum incur late fees; in a worst-case scenario they may forfeit their aid for the first academic period, be unable to get needed books in time to do well in their classes, and be unable to register for the following session or transfer because of their unpaid bill.

Chapter 8
Other Financial Aid Sources

There are many other sources of financial aid that may be available to a student and their families. Many colleges provide scholarships (free money) for students that attend their institutions. Generally this will require a little effort on the student's part. This effort could include researching what scholarships are available, which ones the student qualifies for, writing essays, and gathering letters of recommendation. If the scholarship requires a written essay it is always a good idea to have someone else proofread the student's work before handing it in.

It would be a great idea to check with the college Foundation Office or Financial Aid Office to see what types of scholarships are available for the student; many times this information is available online, along with the application process. Other scholarships may come from your employer or the student's employer. You should contact the Human Resource office where you are employed or check your company website.

Many states also have free grant money for you to attend college. For example New York State has the Tuition Assistance Program (TAP). This grant pays students up to $5,000 per year based on financial need and is available for full-time and part-time students. You should check with your appropriate state agency to see what may be available for the student and learn the criteria for each type of benefit. The agency website is always the best place to begin, but high school counselors and the college financial aid office should also have information.

Grandparents also can be another source of funding. In my years in financial aid I have met with many grandparents that were willing to help pay for the grandchild's education. If there is a grandparent in the family willing and able to help, you should include them in your college decision discussions. You may be pleasantly surprised that they are more than willing to help out with the everrising cost of tuition.

Finally, colleges hope to attract top students and know it is a competitive environment. Many colleges have endowed scholarships that they may offer to the best and brightest students or the top performers in athletics or the arts. If you are the parent of one of these students, colleges may have already offered attractive financial aid packages to your student. In many cases you will be able to compare offers they have received and use those offers as a negotiation instrument to help secure a better financial aid package.

Remember, the highest offer may not equal the lowest out-of-pocket expense, so compare costs as well as financial aid and note how much of the offer is in the form of student loans. In this scenario the student has the advantage because every college wants the best and brightest. Ask about renewable scholarships and consider costs over a four to five year period. Your child will not be happy if they can only afford one year at their school of choice.

Chapter 9
After Day One

Getting through the first billing cycle of the first year can be intimidating. Unfortunately, your involvement doesn't stop there. The FAFSA must be filed every year, as do scholarship applications, which means more deadlines. Don't let your student miss these deadlines!

Students can lose their right to receive aid the following year if they don't perform well academically in Year 1, so your job as a parent is to watch for signs the student is struggling, and do what you can to support them early, before they get too far behind.

Your support might mean encouraging the student to cut back hours at work, reducing home responsibilities, helping them eat healthy meals, helping with extra costs for tutors, getting medical help when needed, helping with transportation issues or laundry; in short, the same things you did for them when they were in high school. Only, this time they may be a lot more appreciative – as long as you have learned the art of parenting your adult child from a bit more distance, a skill that requires patience and practice.

Students who panic and drop classes mid-semester may find themselves owing financial aid money back to the school before they can enroll for the next round of classes. Teach them to get help and advice from their school professionals early; their financial aid and academic advisors, professors, and the many support systems available at every school are there to help them succeed. Remember, due to FERPA privacy laws, if your student does run into such issues, you will not be successful calling to find out why they are not registered, or why they have a bill the following year.

For this reason, be sure to keep the lines of communication open. If they are struggling and feel they cannot talk to you honestly about it, their problems could easily snowball out of control

With a little awareness and planning and your invaluable help, your student will have the best opportunity for success in their college endeavor and you, the all-important parent, will have survived your first adventure in the world of higher education and
financial aid!

Endnotes

1. Alboher, M. "When It Comes to Careers, Change Is a Constant", The New York Times, May 1, 2007 edition (http://www.nytimes.com/2007/05/01/business/smallbusiness/01webcareers.html?_r=1&#)
2. "When Your College Student Changes Majors", College Parents of America blog, November 27, 2010 (http://www.collegeparents.org/blog/2010/11/27/when-your-college-student-changes-majors)
3. "Funding Your Education", The Guide to Federal Student Aid, U.S. Department of Education Office of Federal Student Aid (https://studentaid.ed.gov/sites/default/files/funding-your-education.pdf).
4. "Free Application for Federal Student Aid", U.S. Department of Education Office of Federal Student Aid (https://fafsa.ed.gov/options.htm)
5. "Funding Your Education", The Guide to Federal Student Aid, U.S. Department of Education Office of Federal Student Aid (https://studentaid.ed.gov/sites/default/files/funding-your-education.pdf)
6. "The SmartStudent Guide to Financial Aid", FinAid Page, LLC (http://www.finaid.org/)
7. Smith, J. Y. "Former R.I. Senator Claiborne Pell, 90; Sponsored Grant Program", Washington Post, January 2, 2009 (http://www.washingtonpost.com/wp-dyn/content/article/2009/01/01/AR2009010101521.html)

8. "Student Loan Debt Exceeds One Trillion Dollars", NPR "All Things Considered", April 24, 2012, Mark Kantrowitz interview by Melissa Block (http://www.npr.org/2012/04/24/151305380/student-loan-debt-exceeds-one-trillion-dollars)
9. "Money Essentials", http://money.cnn.com/magazines/moneymag/money101/
10. Larkin, Karen Y. "Average Credit Card Debt for a College Student", http://creditcards.lovetoknow.com/Average_Credit_Card_Debt_for_a_College_Student

Additional Resources

U.S. Department of Education "The Guide to Federal Student Aid - Funding Your Education" Washington D.C. 2014
https://studentaid.ed.gov/resources.

New York State Higher Education Services Corporation (HESC), "Financial Aid Nights" Albany, New York 12246.
http://www.hesc.ny.gov/partner-access/high-school-counselors/financial-aid-nights.html

SUNY Smart Track "Empowered Financial Planning
https://fa.financialavenue.org/suny-home/

CPSIA information can be obtained at www.ICGtesting.com
Printed in the USA
LVOW12s0905150415

434672LV00001B/2/P